Kenwood Elementary Media Center
Kearney, Nebraska
WITHDRAWN

D1261740

534487

Basketballs /
688.7 Bla

Blaxland, Wendy.

Kenwood Media Center

How Are They Made?

Basketballs

Wendy Blaxland

Marshall Cavendish
Benchmark

New York

Kenwood Elementary Media Center
Kearney Nebraska

This edition first published in 2010 in the United States of America by
MARSHALL CAVENDISH BENCHMARK
An imprint of Marshall Cavendish Corporation

All rights reserved.

No part of this publication may be reproduced, stored in a retrieval system or transmitted, in any form or by any means, electronic, mechanical, photocopying, recording, or otherwise, without the prior permission of the copyright owner. Request for permission should be addressed to the Publisher, Marshall Cavendish Corporation, 99 White Plains Road, Tarrytown, NY 10591. Tel: (914) 332-8888, fax: (914) 332-1888.

Website: www.marshallcavendish.us

This publication represents the opinions and views of the author based on Wendy Blaxland's personal experience, knowledge, and research. The information in this book serves as a general guide only. The author and publisher have used their best efforts in preparing this book and disclaim liability rising directly and indirectly from the use and application of this book.

Other Marshall Cavendish Offices:
Marshall Cavendish Ltd. 5th Floor, 32-38 Saffron Hill, London EC1N 8 FH, UK • Marshall Cavendish International (Asia) Private Limited, 1 New Industrial Road, Singapore 536196 • Marshall Cavendish International (Thailand) Co Ltd. 253 Asoke, 12th Flr, Sukhumvit 21 Road, Klongtoey Nua, Wattana, Bangkok 10110, Thailand • Marshall Cavendish (Malaysia) Sdn Bhd, Times Subang, Lot 46, Subang Hi-Tech Industrial Park, Batu Tiga, 40000 Shah Alam, Selangor Darul Ehsan, Malaysia

Marshall Cavendish is a trademark of Times Publishing Limited

All websites were available and accurate when this book was sent to press.

Library of Congress Cataloging-in-Publication Data

Blaxland, Wendy.
    Basketballs / Wendy Blaxland.
       p. cm. — (How are they made?)
    Includes index.
    Summary: "Discusses how basketballs are made"—Provided by publisher.
    ISBN 978-0-7614-4751-1
    1. Basketballs—Design and construction—Juvenile literature. I. Title.
    TS2301.S7B53 2011
688.7'6323--dc22
                                                    2009039874

First published in 2010 by
MACMILLAN EDUCATION AUSTRALIA PTY LTD
15–19 Claremont Street, South Yarra 3141

Visit our website at www.macmillan.com.au or go directly to www.macmillanlibrary.com.au

Associated companies and representatives throughout the world.

Copyright © Wendy Blaxland 2010

Edited by Anna Fern
Text and cover design by Cristina Neri, Canary Graphic Design
Page layout by Peggy Bampton, Relish Graphic
Photo research by Jes Senbergs
Map by Damien Demaj, DEMAP; modified by Cristina Neri, Canary Graphic Design

Printed in the United States

Acknowledgments
The author would like to thank the following for their expert advice: Marcos Beltrà, FIBA, International Basketball Federation, Geneva, Switzerland; Ross Faulkner, Victoria; Michael Haynes, Basketball Australia, Sydney, Australia; Crystal Meadows, Spalding; UN Statistics Division – Economics Statistics Branch, New York, United States.

The author and the publisher are grateful to the following for permission to reproduce copyright material:

Front cover photograph: A stack of basketballs, Palto/istockphoto

Photographs courtesy of:
AAP/AP/Phil Coate, **14**; eStock Photo/Alamy, **4**; Bettman/Corbis, **6**; © James Leynse/Corbis, **22**; © David Maxwell/epa/Corbis, **5** (top); © Katy Winn/Corbis, **27**; Rob Cruse, **8**, **25**; Frederic J. Brown/AFP/Getty Images, **7**; Dorling Kindersley/Getty Images, **11**; Streeter Lecka/Getty Images, **26**; Joe Murphy/Getty Images, **10**; Michael Rosenfeld/Getty Images, **18**; Catherine Steenkeste/Getty Images, **24**; Terrence Vaccaro/Getty Images, **21**; iStockphoto, **3**, **6**, **12**, **17** (left), **29** (bottom); C. M. C. Derm/iStockphoto, **28**; R. B. Freid/iStockphoto, **30**; Chad McDermott/iStockphoto, **28**; Palto/iStockphoto, **19** (bottom); © Ambient Images Inc/Alamy/Photolibrary, **23**; © David Ball/Alamy/Photolibrary, **29** (top); © Nigel Cattlin/Alamy/Photolibrary, **16**; © Greenshoots Communications/Alamy/Photolibrary, **17** (right); © Jim West/Alamy/Photolibrary, **19** (top); Paul Rapson/Science Photo Library/Photolibrary, **9**; Wikipedia, **20**.

While every care has been taken to trace and acknowledge copyright, the publisher tenders their apologies for any accidental infringement where copyright has proved untraceable. Where the attempt has been unsuccessful, the publisher welcomes information that would redress the situation.

1 3 5 6 4 2

Contents

Glossary Words

When a word is printed in **bold**, you can look up its meaning in the Glossary on page 31.

From Raw Materials to Products

Everything we use is made from raw materials from Earth. These are called natural resources. People take natural resources and make them into useful products.

Basketballs

Basketballs are large balls used to play the game of basketball. They are filled with air so they can be bounced, thrown, and caught. The main raw materials used to make basketballs are leather, rubber, and plastic.

Inside the ball is a rubber **bladder**, which holds air. The rubber is made from the sap of certain trees, or from **butyl rubber**, a form of plastic. The bladder is covered with an **elastic** inner body called a **winding**, made of long plastic threads, which come from **petrochemicals**. The winding is enclosed in a basketball cover constructed from leather, rubber, or plastic. Leather is made from animal skin which has been treated so it will last.

Different basketballs are made from different materials.

Why Do We Need Basketballs?

A basketball is the most important piece of equipment in the game of basketball. The ball is tossed from player to player, bounced, and thrown through a round metal hoop.

There are slightly different indoor and outdoor basketballs that are used on the different surfaces.

People of varying ages all around the world play basketball. It is an important game at school and at many colleges. **Professional players** are very well paid and many people admire them and look up to them. Millions of people around the world also enjoy watching basketball games, either live or on television.

LeBron James of the Cleveland Cavaliers goes up for a breakaway dunk.

Question & Answer

What is the fastest growing sport for athletes with disabilities?

Basketball!

5

The History of Basketballs

Basketball was invented in the United States in 1891 by James Naismith, a sports coach. He wanted to create a game of skill that college students could play in a small space indoors during the winter. The first basketball game was played with a soccer ball and two peach baskets.

The inventor of basketball, James Naismith, carrying a ball and a basket used in early games of basketball.

Basketballs through the Ages

1891
James Naismith invents basketball.

January 20, 1892
The first officially recognized game of basketball is played with two teams of nine players on a court half the size of a modern one.

1936
Basketball is introduced at the Berlin Olympics.

1937
Butyl rubber is developed.

1942
Basketballs are first shaped by **molds** in factories to make them the same size and shape.

1890 CE

1894

1920

1930

1940

1950

1894
Spalding develops the first manufactured basketball. It is made from panels of leather stitched together, with a rubber bladder inside a cloth lining.

1924
The International Women's Sports Federation includes a basketball competition.

1946
The first wheelchair basketball games are played by disabled ex-World War II soldiers.

6

Wheelchair basketball is now an Olympic sport.

2004
The U.S. men's basketball team is defeated in the Olympics for the first time since paid players were allowed to compete in 1992.

1967–1976
The American Basketball Association uses a red, white, and blue basketball.

1972
The first **synthetic** basketball is developed.

1950s
Orange balls are introduced because they are easy to see.

1980s
Television coverage leads to an explosion of interest in basketball.

1992
Composite leather basketballs are developed.

1960

1970

1980

1990

2000

Guess What!

In 2007, there were approximately 300 million basketballs in America.

What Are Basketballs Made From?

Basketball covers may be made of leather or a composite leather, rubber, or synthetic rubber for **durability** and feel. Inside the cover is a stretchy bladder into which air is pumped. This bladder is usually made of **latex** or butyl rubber, which gives the ball bounce. The bladder is given its shape by a winding made of long strands of plastic, such as nylon or polyester, wrapped around it. Inks, plastic printed decals, or stickers are used to decorate the surface of the basketball and give information about the ball and its maker. The basketball may also have metallic foil pressed into it.

Question & Answer

What is a particularly bad shot in basketball called?

A brick.

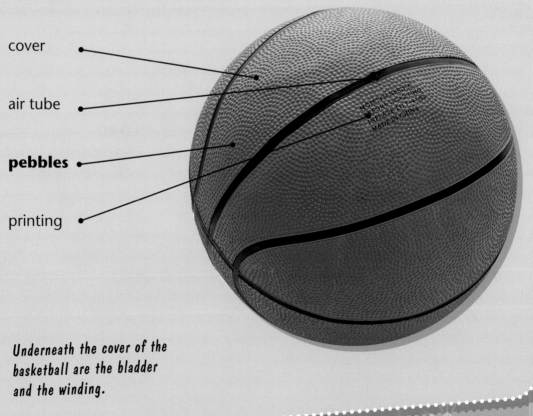

cover

air tube

pebbles

printing

Underneath the cover of the basketball are the bladder and the winding.

Materials

Many different materials are used to make basketballs. As with the making of all products, energy is also used to run the machines which help mine the oil and gas for synthetic materials, process the rubber and leather, and put the basketballs together.

Synthetic materials, such as butyl rubber and plastic, are made in chemical factories.

Materials Used to Make Basketballs

Material	Purpose and Qualities
Leather	Used to make top-grade basketball covers. Gives a soft, durable surface that is easy to grip.
Composite leather	Looks and feels like leather, but is less expensive.
Microfiber	A material made from plastic that has been woven into synthetic fibers. It is used in basketball covers.
Latex rubber	Used to make bladders. Latex rubber bladders stretch and allow a ball to bounce, but air slowly seeps from them.
Butyl rubber	Also used to make bladders. Butyl rubber stretches, is durable, and retains air well.
Plastic	Used to make the winding, which gives the ball its shape. Plastic is cheap, strong, and can be made into threads to wrap around the bladder.
Ink, foil	Used to decorate the basketball surface and print information on it.

Basketball Design

There are **regulations** about the design of basketballs used in competitions. Each basketball organization insists that balls must be the same standard weight and size and often of a certain color and material. The balls must also bounce to a particular height and be inflated to a certain pressure. Many organizations insist, as well, that balls are free of poisonous materials, heavy metals, and substances that may cause allergic reactions.

Indoor basketballs are generally made of leather. Outdoor basketballs, which need to be tougher to cope with **asphalt** and gravel surfaces, are usually made of rubber. Indoor/outdoor balls, which are very common, are generally constructed from long-lasting composite materials, and sometimes of rubber.

National Basketball Association (NBA) regulation basketballs are made from leather by the Spalding company.

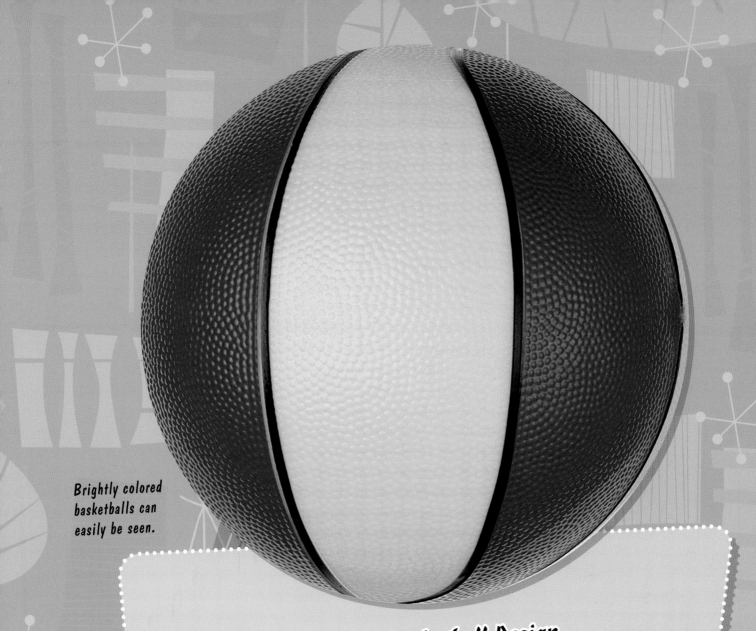

Brightly colored basketballs can easily be seen.

Question & Answer

What color should a basketball be?

There is no standard color. Many competitions, however, insist on balls of a certain color. Most basketballs are orange so that they can be seen easily.

Improving Basketball Design

Basketball **manufacturers** try to improve the design of basketballs with new materials, construction, or decorations. New basketballs are often designed, but they are only made if they are acceptable to players.

Some recent basketballs have dimples to improve the player's grip, or evenly spaced grooves to make the balls bounce the same way every time from every angle. Other balls are made of polyurethane with tiny holes to absorb sweat and make the balls less slippery. Some manufacturers focus on changing the surface color or design, to make basketballs more attractive or visible, or to help teach young players where to put their hands.

From Rubber and Leather to Basketballs

The process of making everyday objects such as basketballs from raw materials involves a number of steps. In the first stage, the leather, rubber, and other materials are prepared. At the second stage, the bladder, winding, and cover of the basketball are made. In the final stage, the basketball is assembled. Finally the ball is finished with printing and **embossing**.

Stage 1: Making Materials for Basketballs

Rubber

Latex is collected from rubber trees. Synthetic rubber is made from chemicals.

↓

The latex or synthetic rubber is heated with chemicals to make it strong and elastic.

Leather

The skins of animals are cleaned.

↓

Next, they are soaked in chemicals to make them **flexible** and waterproof. This is called tanning.

Other materials, such as plastic and fabric, may be used to make basketball covers.

Stage 2: Making the Bladder, Winding, and Cover

Bladder

The bladder is cut from sheets of butyl rubber and a hole is cut for the air tube.

↓

The air tube is inserted. Then the bladder is sealed with heat and treated with chemicals to make it strong and elastic.

↓

Next, the bladder is filled with air.

↓

The winding, made of many strands of nylon or polyester thread, is wrapped around the bladder to make a strong, well-shaped ball.

Cover

The shapes of the pieces for the cover are cut from leather, composite leather, rubber, or plastic.

↓

A hole is cut in one piece for the air tube.

↓

The shaped pieces are joined to form a cover. Leather pieces are stitched together. Rubber, synthetic rubber, and plastic are fused or melted together.

Stage 3: Finishing Basketballs

The winding is glued to the cover.

↓

Next, the cover is decorated with printed information.

↓

Then the basketball's surface is embossed with pebbles.

↓

Next, the basketball is inspected and tested to see that it bounces well enough.

↓

Lastly, the basketball is **deflated**, ready for packing.

Guess What!

A circus shot is one shot that is flipped, heaved, scooped, or flung toward the hoop while the shooter is off-balance, airborne, facing away from the basket, or falling down.

Kenwood Elementary Media Center
Kearney Nebraska

Raw Materials for Basketballs

The major raw materials for basketballs are leather, rubber, and different plastics. The traditional materials of leather and rubber are still used for making most basketballs because they are cheaper.

Leather is produced in a wide range of countries. More than half of the world's rubber is now produced synthetically, but natural rubber is grown in hot areas near the equator. Rubber for basketball covers comes mostly from Thailand and Vietnam.

The different plastics used to make basketballs are all made from oil and gas produced by the petrochemical industry in the United States, western Europe, the Middle East, and Asia.

Water basketball is a skilled and energetic game.

ARCTIC OCEAN

NORTH AMERICA
United States of America ❗

ATLANTIC OCEAN

Brazil ◎

SOUTH AMERICA

Guess What!

Water basketball is played in various countries, with different numbers of players. Countries disagree on where to put the basket, and whether or not it should float.

Centers for Basketball Production

Most basketballs are now produced in large factories in China. Basketballs for professional teams are also made in Taiwan and Thailand, and many inexpensive basketballs come from India. Factories usually produce basketballs for only a few weeks each year. The rest of the year they make other sorts of sports balls. The different parts of basketballs are generally produced in the same factory, where the raw materials are all brought together.

This map shows countries that are important to the production of basketballs.

Key

✛ Important rubber-producing countries

✪ Important leather-producing countries

❗ Important oil- and gas-producing countries

◉ Important basketball-producing countries

Russian Federation ✪ ❗

ASIA

EUROPE

Italy ✪

Iran ❗

South Korea ✪

Japan ◉

Saudi Arabia ❗   India ✛ ✪ ✪ ◉

Taiwan ◉

Vietnam ✛ ◉

Thailand ✛ ◉

✛ Malaysia

Indonesia ✛

PACIFIC OCEAN

ATLANTIC OCEAN

INDIAN OCEAN

Stage 1: Making Materials for Basketballs

Different materials for basketballs come from animals, plants, and minerals.

Rubber

Natural rubber is made from latex, a gum collected from rubber trees. Workers make a shallow cut in the bark and leave a small cup to collect the oozing gum. The rubber is heated with other substances, such as sulfur, to make it harder and more elastic and to stop it **decaying**. This is called **vulcanization**.

Butyl rubber is often used in making basketball bladders. This is a synthetic rubber made from petrochemicals in factories. Butyl rubber is also vulcanized by sulfur.

Guess What!

NBA star Yao Ming has become a United Nations Environmental Champion to raise awareness of climate change and environmental issues.

A sticky sap called latex is drained from trees to make natural rubber for basketballs.

Leather

Leather is made from the skins of animals, mainly cattle. The process of turning the skins into leather is called tanning.

The skins are first cleaned and salted to stop them rotting. They are then tanned, which involves soaking the skins in special chemicals called tannins. Tanning is done with either metal or vegetable tannins and can take up to a year.

After tanning, the leather is washed, split to the right thickness, oiled, and dyed. It is then stretched and dried. Finally, the leather is brushed and polished.

Sometimes composite leather is used in making basketballs. Leather is cut up and mixed with other materials, such as plastic, on a backing made of fabric.

Animal skins are stretched on frames to dry during the tanning process.

Stage 2: Making the Bladder, Winding, and Cover

The bladder, winding, and cover are all constructed separately.

Making the Bladder and Winding

To make the bladder, black butyl rubber is melted and made into a sheet. Next, a hole is punched in the sheet to hold the air tube, and the sheet is bonded to the air tube. It is then punch-cut into a round shape and the edges are melted together. Next, the bladder is heated and filled with air in a vulcanizer, which makes the rubber stronger, more flexible, and more durable. Bladders are tested to make sure the air does not escape.

The air-filled bladders are then taken to the winding department. The winding around the bladder consists of many very long strands of polyester or nylon thread. This makes the ball strong and well shaped. Almost 1.9 miles (3 kilometers) of thread are used in one basketball.

The bladder of the basketball is made from sheets of black butyl rubber.

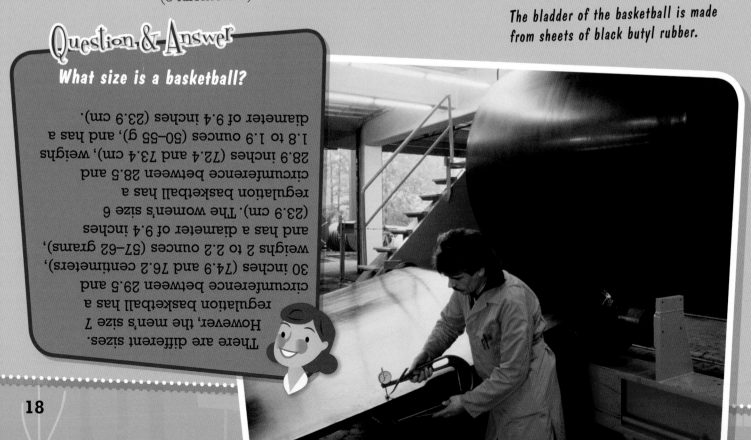

Question & Answer

What size is a basketball?

There are different sizes. However, the men's size 7 regulation basketball has a circumference between 29.5 and 30 inches (74.9 and 76.2 centimeters), weighs 2 to 2.2 ounces (57–62 grams), and has a diameter of 9.4 inches (23.9 cm). The women's size 6 regulation basketball has a circumference between 28.5 and 28.9 inches (72.4 and 73.4 cm), weighs 1.8 to 1.9 ounces (50–55 g), and has a diameter of 9.4 inches (23.9 cm).

Leather panels for covers are carefully stitched together by machine.

Making the Cover

The basketball covers are made separately from the bladder and winding. Each cover consists of six panels. First, the panel outlines are printed on a roll of leather, rubber, or plastic. Then a punch press machine cuts out the panels and the opening for the air tube. Scraps are recycled.

Next, the panels are fitted together. Rubber or plastic panels are placed in a machine which holds them, creates the channels and adds any embossed information. Leather panels are stitched together by a heavy-duty sewing machine.

Stage 3: Finishing Basketballs

The bladder, wrapped in the winding, is now put together with the basketball cover.

Assembling Basketballs

The bladder and winding of a rubber ball are coated with glue and put in a vulcanizer lined with the cover panel. The vulcanizer uses heat to bond the cover to the winding. The bladder and winding are inserted into leather or plastic covers.

These molds are used to emboss pebbles and channels into the basketball surface.

Question & Answer

How many pebbles does a standard basketball have on its surface?

A standard basketball has approximately 3,500 to 4,100 pebbles. Each pebble has a diameter of 0.1 inches (2.5 millimeters).

Finishing Basketballs

The decals, printed information, and foil decoration are pressed on the surface of the ball by hand with small heat presses. Then the balls are inspected. Any gaps between the panels of rubber balls are filled in and the ball is vulcanized again. Finally, the surface of the basketball is embossed with pebbles.

The balls are tested to make sure they are airtight at each stage. Then they are bounce-tested to make sure they bounce high enough, and the printing is inspected. Lastly, the basketballs are deflated, ready for packing.

Becoming the official basketball manufacturer for a major organization brings a company sales and prestige.

Packaging and Distribution

Products are packaged to protect them while they are being transported. Packaging also shows the maker's brand and makes products look attractive when they are displayed for sale.

Air is let out of basketballs so they take less space to pack and transport. Basketballs are generally packaged in polyethylene plastic bags. These are then put in bulk boxes to be sent to **distributors**. The distributors can then reinflate the balls to the right pressure and pack them separately into display boxes, usually made of cardboard, for sale. The display boxes may also be packed in bulk boxes or cartons, which are often shrink-wrapped.

After shipping from the factory to the distributor, basketballs are inflated and packed into boxes ready to be sold.

This store in New York sells regulation NBA basketballs and clothing.

Distribution

Basketballs must be shipped from where they are made to where they are sold, often in other countries. Manufacturers generally send basketballs in large numbers to distributors, who have the right to sell them in a certain area.

Distributors sell the basketballs to **retailers**, such as sports goods stores, toy stores, and department and chain stores, which then sell them to individuals. Distributors also sell basketballs directly in bulk to sports clubs and schools. Some basketballs can be bought directly from the manufacturer over the Internet or by mail.

Question & Answer

How are basketballs tested?

Some sports companies use a machine that gives a basketball a five-minute workout equal to what it would get in a full-length game. To do this, the ball is pushed down a chute, which launches it at a backboard at about 30 miles (48 km) per hour. It then bounces back into the chute. Balls are also tested for bounce and deflation.

23

Marketing and Advertising

Marketing and advertising are used to **promote** and sell products.

Marketing

Basketballs are used in a popular game, so they are marketed as part of the sport. Clubs and schools play in competitions arranged by organizations, which generally have strict rules about which sort of basketball can be used, and often require a particular company.

Basketballs sold to individuals playing for fun are advertised by price or appearance, or their association with well-known players. Basketballs aimed at professional players are marketed according to how they feel and handle, their ability to stay inflated, and their reliability.

Shaquille O'Neal unveils a huge billboard of himself for the opening of a basketball store in Los Angeles.

Guess What!

The tallest basketball player ever was probably Libyan player Suleiman Ali Nashnush at 8 feet 0.5 inches (245 cm) tall. Sun Ming Ming, at 7 feet 9 inches (236 cm) tall, is the tallest basketball player alive.

Advertising

Basketballs are advertised in magazines and on websites dedicated to sports and basketball. They may be advertised as part of a sports store promotion, or as part of holiday promotions. Advertising campaigns may also be timed for when teams begin their year's playing season.

Advertising basketballs, basketball shoes, and clothes often depends heavily on linking the products with certain teams or well-known players. Mini-basketballs are used to advertise the sport, and are often given away. Objects such as watches and lights made in the shape of basketballs advertise basketballs indirectly, too. Basketball players may also be paid to help advertise other goods, such as sneakers or soda.

Advertising in specialized magazines can target buyers very interested in basketball.

Production of Basketballs

Huge quantities of products can be made in factories. This is called mass production. They may also be constructed by hand in small quantities by skilled craftspeople. Most basketballs are mass-produced, although some are custom-made.

Mass Production

Big factories produce basketballs as part of a range of other sports balls such as footballs and soccer balls. Large companies compete to become the official manufacturer of basketballs for college or professional competitions. This way they will sell large quantities of basketballs, and often other products, such as souvenir T-shirts.

Earl Boykins of the Charlotte Bobcats is only 5 feet 5 inches tall. Even though he is shorter than most professional players, he is very good at basketball.

Small-Scale Production

Some specially designed basketballs may be produced only in small numbers. They can be used to promote a certain team or advertise a particular competition, and often have different information printed on them.

A number of novelty basketballs are produced. They might have unusual colors, metallic finishes, or even be glow-in-the-dark, with holders for replaceable light sticks. Mini-basketballs are also used to promote the game or other products.

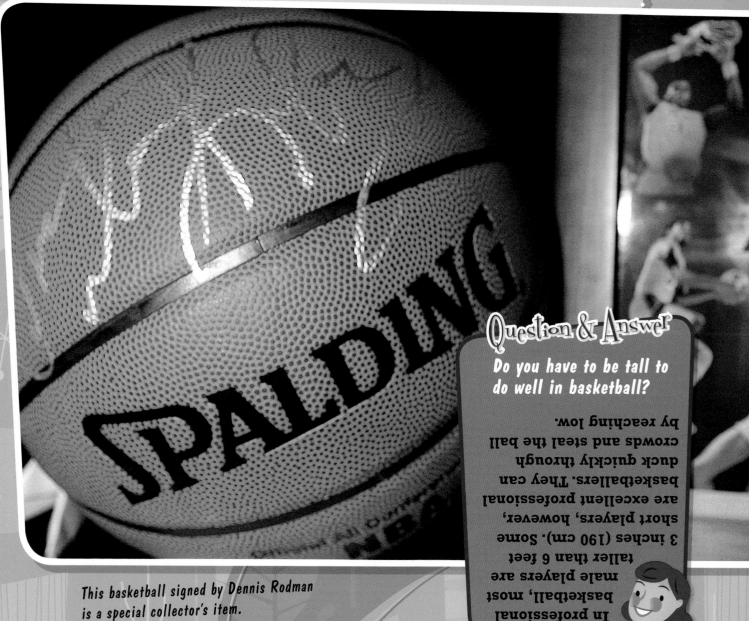

This basketball signed by Dennis Rodman is a special collector's item.

Question & Answer

Do you have to be tall to do well in basketball?

In professional basketball, most male players are taller than 6 feet 3 inches (190 cm). Some short players, however, are excellent professional basketballers. They can duck quickly through crowds and steal the ball by reaching low.

Basketballs and the Environment

The oil being processed at this refinery is a nonrenewable resource.

Making any product affects the environment. It also affects the people who make the product. It is important to think about the impact of a product through its entire life cycle. This includes getting the raw materials, making the product, and disposing of it. Any problems need to be worked on so products can be made in the best ways possible.

Renewable and Nonrenewable Materials

Plastic for basketballs is made from oil and natural gas. These are **nonrenewable resources**, so it is important to recycle basketballs when possible. It is also important to find **renewable** sources of materials, such as plant-based plastics. Rubber and leather are renewable materials, although raising cattle for leather uses many valuable land resources.

Factory Workers

Some companies making basketballs have employed underage workers, used unsafe working practices, and paid unfair wages. However, many countries have laws to stop these problems, and responsible companies make sure their basketballs are made using fair practices.

This garbage dump is piled high with plastic that will not rot away.

Recycling

Scrap rubber and leather from making basketballs can be used again. At least one company is making a basketball from 40 percent recycled rubber.

Plastic can be recycled, but a large amount of plastic is thrown away because people are confused about which plastic types are recyclable. Plastic does not decay, which can create a pollution problem. In 2008, however, scientists discovered two kinds of plastic-eating bacteria that can consume plastic in three months.

Guess What!

A company called Fair Trade Sports produces a basketball called "Respect." It is guaranteed to have been made by workers who are treated fairly.

Questions to Think About

We need to conserve the raw materials used to produce even ordinary objects such as basketballs. Recycling materials such as rubber and plastic from basketballs, conserving energy, and preventing pollution as much as possible means there will be enough resources in the future and a cleaner environment.

These are some questions you might like to think about:

* Do you think rubber, leather, or plastic basketballs are best for the environment? Why?

* How can basketballs be recycled in your school or community?

* What does your favorite basketball look like?

* Can you think of a better surface for basketballs than pebbling?

* What is the most important feature of your favorite basketball?

* How do you think basketballs can be improved?

What does your favorite basketball look like?

Glossary

asphalt
Black, cement-like material for paving the ground.

bladder
Airtight, elastic container.

butyl rubber
A synthetic rubber made from petrochemicals.

composite leather
Synthetic leather made from several materials.

decaying
Gradually breaking down.

deflated
Having the air taken out.

distributors
Sellers of large quantities of goods that have the right to sell a particular product in a certain area.

durability
Able to last a long time.

elastic
Easily stretched and able to return to original shape.

embossing
A raised pattern pressed into the surface as decoration.

flexible
Able to bend.

latex
Gum collected from rubber trees.

manufacturers
Makers, usually with machines in factories.

molds
Hollow forms in which materials can be shaped to make objects.

nonrenewable resources
Resources that cannot easily be replaced once they run out.

pebbles
Tiny regular rounded bumps on the surface of a basketball to help the player grip it.

petrochemicals
Chemicals made from petroleum, oil, or natural gas.

professional players
People who earn a living playing basketball.

promote
Conduct an advertising campaign in order to sell goods.

regulations
Official rules.

renewable
Something that can easily be grown or made again.

retailers
Stores that sell products to individual customers.

synthetic
Made by humans, often using petrochemicals.

United Nations
An international organization that works on issues affecting all people and countries.

vulcanization
Treatment of rubbery materials with heat and chemicals to make them stronger, stretchier, or longer lasting.

winding
An elastic cover that gives strength and shape to a basketball bladder.

Index